# The
# LAW of
# BIBLICAL
# MECHANICS

# The LAW of BIBLICAL MECHANICS

## PRINCIPLES AND PROCESSES FOR MANAGEMENT AND STEWARDSHIP

---

### Ernest R. Roberts III
#### PE, PMP

Published by Roberts Consulting Engineers, PLLC, Matteson, Illinois.

ISBN paperback: 979-8-9905888-0-6
ISBN ebook: 979-8-9905888-1-3
Library of Congress Control Number: 2024909664




Cover design by Howard Grossman.

This book is dedicated to my parents,
*Ernest Roberts II and Ruth Roberts,*
who provided me a clear path for success and
a stable household and community in which to flourish,
along with strong moral and biblical principles.

# CONTENTS

# INTRODUCTION

One of the most difficult leadership positions in any organization is that of project manager. There are many things to keep track of: scope, schedule, budget, meetings, team development, quality control, stakeholder coordination, risk management, and on and on. Companies rise or fall based on this critical position, and the larger the team, scope, and budget, the more overwhelming the job can feel.

In my thirty-plus-year career, which includes my work as a licensed Professional Engineer (PE) and a certified Project Management Professional (PMP), I've run into numerous issues that required me to think quickly on my feet. Over time, I realized that the Bible holds many principles that would help me succeed more quickly and easily in those situations, principles that would allow me far more success in every area of my life.

Ephesians 4:11 speaks of the "five-fold ministry"—the five roles God has called Christians to fulfill: apostle, prophet, evangelist, pastor, and teacher. My "gifting" aligns most closely to teacher, as I enjoy mastering concepts, breaking down complex topics and ideas into their most basic elements, and applying knowledge to everyday situations. In this book I will share some of my thoughts about management and biblical principles, including my analysis of Bible verses and practical applications of their lessons. My goal is to offer you something to think about as you deal with project management and as you try to understand the purpose of humanity. I trust you will find some tool or concept that you can apply to your business, organization, or family to enhance your giftings and talents in your chosen area of influence.

I will be referencing the New King James Version of the Bible (NKJV) as well as *A Guide to the Project Management Body of Knowledge* (known as the *PMBOK®️ Guide*).

## LEVELS OF RESPONSIBILITY

To set some context, I want to make a distinction between technical, management, and leadership roles, or levels of responsibility.

The technical level, or the level of implementation, is the lowest level of responsibility. Now don't misunderstand me: we need this level to get things done, as it includes subject matter experts, but usually this level is charged with carrying out orders from higher up in the organization.

The next level, management, is usually charged with helping organize the implementation of a project or task and making sure the various aspects of implementation work together.

Leadership, however, is on a totally different level. A leader has vision; a leader sees the big picture and creates processes and principles that can then be filtered down to the project team, so that everyone ultimately benefits. A leader is also one who is self-sacrificing. In other words, a leader cannot ask anyone to do anything that he or she is not willing to do or is not already in the process of doing.

## DEFINITIONS

It is important to establish some definitions for the purpose of this book.

**Analysis.** The breakdown of a subject to its most basic elements.

**Anointing.** The ritual act of pouring oil, such as in a religious ceremony; a ceremonial blessing. The empowerment to prosper granted by the creator of the universe (God), even though it is not earned (in other words, it is given through grace). Also, the ability to override time, space, and matter to achieve a result or outcome.

**Discernment.** The ability to judge or perceive something that is not obvious. Also, spiritual guidance and understanding that supersedes human knowledge and understanding.

**Integrity.** The quality of being honest and having strong moral principles; moral uprightness; staying true to strong values and beliefs even when it's unpopular, inconvenient, or unseen. Also, a state of completeness or wholeness.

**Law.** A statement of fact, based on the observation that a particular phenomenon always occurs given a certain set of conditions; for example, the law of gravity. A rule or set of rules defining correct procedure or behavior, generally enforced by society either formally or informally. An established truth.

**Management.** Supervising or conducting the activity of an entity, such as an organization or a project team; the activity that directs group efforts to accomplish specific goals. Also, the ability to work effectively with and through others to achieve the goals of the organization or project.

**Mechanics.** The branch of science that deals with the relationship between force, motion, and objects. Also, the functional details of how something works, such as the mechanics of the human body.

**Parable.** A short story that illustrates a lesson or principle, often used in reference to stories told by Jesus in the Bible.

**Principle.** A fundamental law, truth, or assumption that is the foundation for a system of belief or a chain of reasoning. A rule or belief that governs behavior; a code of conduct.

**Process.** A series of actions or steps that lead to a particular end—for example, the making of a product.

**Project.** An endeavor undertaken to create a unique product, service, or result; it has a defined beginning and end, a specific scope, and assigned resources.

**Stewardship.** The judicious management of something entrusted to one's care, such as property, financial affairs, or an estate.

## POINTS TO PONDER

Before we get into the discussion of biblical mechanics, I want to leave you with a few thoughts to consider and to keep in mind as you read.

We've all occasionally said, "I've heard that one before" and turned away from the teaching. I ask you to consider, though: if you know something, what are the results of your "knowing"? Have you internalized the lesson, or is it a superficial knowing? We can easily be deceived into thinking that we know something we don't. As James 1:22–25 says:

[22] But be doers of the word, and not hearers only, deceiving yourselves. [23] For if anyone is a hearer of the word and not a doer, he is like a man observing his natural face in a mirror; [24] for he observes himself, goes

away, and immediately forgets what kind of man he was. [25] But he who looks into the perfect law of liberty and continues in it, and is not a forgetful hearer but a doer of the work, this one will be blessed in what he does.

And as Romans 10:17 reminds us, "faith comes by hearing, and hearing by the word of God."

As you take in the lessons here, ask yourself: *Will my current doctrines and principles help me have a better life and get me where I want to go?* Perhaps yes. But if not, toss them out and consider new ones. In each chapter, I share biblical and personal examples that show how and where the various principles work.

Many laws and principles—say, the law of gravity or the law of electricity—have made the human experience vastly more tolerable and even enjoyable. But misuse or ignorance of these same laws or principles could harm or even kill you. Essentially, the same applies to the principles I discuss here: use them for good, not evil.

We each have a responsibility to steward our business and personal lives so that we can leave a legacy to future generations. I hope I am able to teach readers how God has empowered humankind to succeed and prosper using biblical mechanics. But my audience is broad, so I hope that whatever your belief system, you will be able to see the wisdom presented and reconsider not only standard project management practices but biblical principles as well.

Now sit back, relax, and let's enjoy this journey together.

# PRINCIPLE 1: PURPOSE

*We must understand our mandate.*
*We must understand our purpose,*
*whether in life or on a project, because when*
*we don't understand it, we go off-track.*

## THE BIBLICAL PERSPECTIVE

Management and stewardship go back well over 6,000 years to the first humans and the first parents, Adam and Eve. They were empowered by the Most High to run the earth and, I believe, ultimately the universe. The scriptures are clear. Genesis 1:26–28 states:

[26] Then God said, "Let Us make man in Our image,

according to Our likeness; let them have dominion over the fish of the sea, over the birds of the air, and over the cattle, over all the earth and over every creeping thing that creeps on the earth." [27] So God created man in His own image; in the image of God He created him; male and female He created them. [28] Then God blessed them, and God said to them, "Be fruitful and multiply; fill the earth and subdue it; have dominion over the fish of the sea, over the birds of the air, and over every living thing that moves on the earth."

As you can see, management and stewardship are in the very DNA of humanity. If you go on to read the entire creation story in the first few chapters of Genesis, Adam didn't go to a big university or trade school to learn how to name the animals or the beasts of the field. He had a "download," if you will, that enabled him to know and name the earth's creatures. Adam didn't learn; he *discerned*. Think of the former as natural, sensory knowledge and the latter as spiritual knowledge. Spiritual knowledge is a powerful gift indeed.

Adam was given what project management theory calls a *project charter*, which gives the project manager (in this case, Adam) the authority to apply organizational resources to project activities and objectives.

## The First Recorded Instance of Mismanagement

We must understand that absolutely nothing in this

world belongs to us. We are only managers and stewards of this world, *not* owners. Adam and Eve had their mandate; all they had to do was to not eat of the tree of knowledge of good and evil (Genesis 2:17).

We are about to go really deep; this will help establish the future chapters on management and stewardship, but for now I'm going to quote Genesis 3:1–24:

[1] Now the serpent was more cunning than any beast of the field which the Lord God had made. And he said to the woman, "Has God indeed said, 'You shall not eat of every tree of the garden'?"

[2] And the woman said to the serpent, "We may eat the fruit of the trees of the garden; [3] but of the fruit of the tree which is in the midst of the garden, God has said, 'You shall not eat it, nor shall you touch it, lest you die.'"

[4] Then the serpent said to the woman, "You will not surely die. [5] For God knows that in the day you eat of it your eyes will be opened, and you will be like God, knowing good and evil."

[6] So when the woman saw that the tree was good for food, that it was pleasant to the eyes, and a tree desirable to make one wise, she took of its fruit and ate. She also gave to her husband with her, and he ate. [7] Then the eyes of both of them were opened, and they knew that they were naked; and they sewed fig leaves together and made themselves coverings.

[8] And they heard the sound of the Lord God walk-

ing in the garden in the cool of the day, and Adam and his wife hid themselves from the presence of the Lord God among the trees of the garden.

[9] Then the Lord God called to Adam and said to him, "Where are you?"

[10] So he said, "I heard Your voice in the garden, and I was afraid because I was naked; and I hid myself."

[11] And He said, "Who told you that you were naked? Have you eaten from the tree of which I commanded you that you should not eat?"

[12] Then the man said, "The woman whom You gave to be with me, she gave me of the tree, and I ate."

[13] And the Lord God said to the woman, "What is this you have done?"

The woman said, "The serpent deceived me, and I ate."

[14] So the Lord God said to the serpent:

> "Because you have done this,
> You are cursed more than all cattle,
> And more than every beast of the field;
> On your belly you shall go,
> And you shall eat dust
> All the days of your life.
> [15] And I will put enmity
> Between you and the woman,
> And between your seed and her seed;
> He shall bruise your head,
> And you shall bruise his heel."

¹⁶ To the woman He said:

> "I will greatly multiply your sorrow and your
> conception;
> In pain you shall bring forth children;
> Your desire shall be for your husband,
> And he shall rule over you."

¹⁷ Then to Adam He said, "Because you have heeded the voice of your wife, and have eaten from the tree of which I commanded you, saying, 'You shall not eat of it':

> "Cursed is the ground for your sake;
> In toil you shall eat of it
> All the days of your life.
> ¹⁸ Both thorns and thistles it shall bring forth for
> you,
> And you shall eat the herb of the field.
> ¹⁹ In the sweat of your face you shall eat bread
> Till you return to the ground,
> For out of it you were taken;
> For dust you are,
> And to dust you shall return."

²⁰ And Adam called his wife's name Eve, because she was the mother of all living.

²¹ Also for Adam and his wife the Lord God made tunics of skin, and clothed them.

<sup></sup>²² Then the Lord God said, "Behold, the man has become like one of Us, to know good and evil. And now, lest he put out his hand and take also of the tree of life, and eat, and live forever"—²³ therefore the Lord God sent him out of the garden of Eden to till the ground from which he was taken. ²⁴ So He drove out the man; and He placed cherubim at the east of the Garden of Eden, and a flaming sword which turned every way, to guard the way to the tree of life.

There is a lot to unpack here, so I will sum this up with the following points:

Adam was the head manager and was created to have headship (he was created before the woman and was given all the instructions and mandates from the Most High). He was responsible for communicating with his wife the plan, vision, and rules that governed their lives and the planet accordingly. The woman (she had not yet been named Eve at this point) was supposed to be his helpmeet and assistant in accomplishing the tasks and requirements.

The woman's responsibility was to tell the serpent that what he was proposing was out of line with the will of God and went against the instructions of her husband. She should have consulted with her husband (the project manager) *before* making such a critical decision.

Adam could have stopped the rebellion underway by reminding his wife that what she did was out of line, but instead he went along with the disobedient act by failing to communicate the severity of the situation. He used a communication method called *avoidance*—that is, *not* communicating. (Anyone familiar with project management and communication styles well knows that this is about the worst form of communication!)

Once the Most High came back to check on the first couple, the blame game began in earnest. Adam blamed the woman, the woman blamed the serpent, and so on. You know the rest of the story: the two were put out of the Garden of Eden with cursings instead of blessings on their lives.

The fall of humanity is where our story really begins. Adam fell from revelation and went into survival mode, and humanity had to be redeemed to God. In my mind, this entire sad episode was a result of poor management skills as well as failure to take responsibility for errors and omissions.

After the Fall, we entered a situation where two systems exist:

+ **The world system:** This system relies on logic, reason, and the five senses (sometimes called "natural knowledge").
+ **The Kingdom of God system:** This system is the one that was widely available to humankind before the Fall.

Every day we have a choice of which system to operate in. In the Kingdom system, Adam could use revelation knowledge, but when he moved to the world system, he had to rely on his natural senses to tell him how to operate. This is a key concept in all the examples in this book illustrating how we choose to deal with various problems and situations. We are *not* to toil for the answer but rather we are to get reconnected to the Creator to receive divine instructions, not only about how to operate correctly but also how to master every situation.

Now let's look at the Enemy of Humanity and how he was able to cause such a disaster. Stay with me, folks. I'm still building my case on management and stewardship.

## The Mystery of Iniquity and the Enemy of Humanity

War, disease, pestilence, racism, failed businesses, failed marriages, economic disaster, early and untimely deaths—each of these has its origin in the Fall. So the question must be asked: *Why did God allow our first parents to be subjected to such assault and temptation when he already knew what the outcome would be?* (The Most High is omniscient and omnipresent, of course.)

I believe the answer is not so elusive as we are led to believe by religion and tradition; rather, it is right under our noses.

Lucifer—also known also as the Devil, the Dragon, the Serpent, and the Accuser of the Brethren, and the god of this world system (though not the god of the earth, as that designation belongs to the Lord God)—was the "anointed cherub angel who covers." We see this in Ezekiel 28:11–19 as follows:

[11] Moreover the word of the Lord came to me, saying, [12] "Son of man, take up a lamentation for the king of Tyre, and say to him, 'Thus says the Lord God:

"You were the seal of perfection,
Full of wisdom and perfect in beauty.
[13] You were in Eden, the garden of God;
Every precious stone was your covering:
The sardius, topaz, and diamond,
Beryl, onyx, and jasper,
Sapphire, turquoise, and emerald with gold.
The workmanship of your timbrels and pipes
Was prepared for you on the day you were created.

[14] "You were the anointed cherub who covers;
I established you;
You were on the holy mountain of God;
You walked back and forth in the midst of fiery stones.
[15] You were perfect in your ways from the day you
    were created,
Till iniquity was found in you.

[16] "By the abundance of your trading
You became filled with violence within,
And you sinned;
Therefore I cast you as a profane thing
Out of the mountain of God;
And I destroyed you, O covering cherub,
From the midst of the fiery stones.

[17] "Your heart was lifted up because of your beauty;
You corrupted your wisdom for the sake of your
    splendor;
I cast you to the ground,
I laid you before kings,
That they might gaze at you.

[18] "You defiled your sanctuaries
By the multitude of your iniquities,
By the iniquity of your trading;
Therefore I brought fire from your midst;
It devoured you,
And I turned you to ashes upon the earth
In the sight of all who saw you.
[19] All who knew you among the peoples are
    astonished at you;
You have become a horror,
And shall be no more forever." ' "

We see in this passage of scripture that Lucifer was not just any ordinary angelic being—his job was to carry the revelation of God to the earth and nature. He obviously got wind that humankind was coming. As we read in Psalms 8:1–9, Lucifer had major objections, as King David records so accurately:

[1] O Lord, our Lord,
How excellent is Your name in all the earth,
Who have set Your glory above the heavens!

2 Out of the mouth of babes and nursing infants
You have ordained strength,
Because of Your enemies,
That You may silence the enemy and the avenger.

3 When I consider Your heavens, the work of Your
    fingers,
The moon and the stars, which You have ordained,
4 What is man that You are mindful of him,
And the son of man that You visit him?
5 For You have made him a little lower than the angels,
And You have crowned him with glory and honor.

6 You have made him to have dominion over the
    works of Your hands;
You have put all things under his feet,
7 All sheep and oxen—
Even the beasts of the field,
8 The birds of the air,
And the fish of the sea
That pass through the paths of the seas.

9 O Lord, our Lord,
How excellent is Your name in all the earth!

So, Lucifer has protested the coming of man. (Can
you imagine telling the god of the universe what he can
and cannot create?) His job was to sing the revelations
of God to the earth and announce the coming of human-

kind to the earth, but instead he did the unthinkable, as we see in Isaiah 14:12–17:

12 "How you are fallen from heaven,
O Lucifer, son of the morning!
How you are cut down to the ground,
You who weakened the nations!
13 For you have said in your heart:
'I will ascend into heaven,
I will exalt my throne above the stars of God;
I will also sit on the mount of the congregation
On the farthest sides of the north;
14 I will ascend above the heights of the clouds,
I will be like the Most High.'
15 Yet you shall be brought down to Sheol,
To the lowest depths of the pit.

16 "Those who see you will gaze at you,
And consider you, saying:
'Is this the man who made the earth tremble,
Who shook kingdoms,
17 Who made the world as a wilderness
And destroyed its cities,
Who did not open the house of his prisoners?'"

So Lucifer falls. He is cast out of heaven and his original position, and, after deceiving Adam and Eve, he has legal authority to dominate this earth and humankind. The Devil himself has now become the god of this world system.

## Satan, the Master Deceiver and Squatter

Satan not only became the god of this world system but also earned squatter's rights against humanity. What do I mean by squatter's rights?

According to earthly law, *squatters' rights*, or *adverse possession*, refers to the rights someone may gain if they occupy a property for a certain period without the owner taking legal action against them. Squatting is a form of trespassing, but it involves the intention of claiming ownership or permanent residency. To remove squatters, property owners must follow a legal eviction process, typically beginning with a call to local law enforcement and the filing of an unlawful detainer action.

After Adam and Eve transgressed divine law in the Garden, Satan become the god of this world and had the power of death. Hebrews 2:14 says:

> Inasmuch then as the children have partaken of flesh and blood, He Himself likewise shared in the same, that through death He might destroy him who *had* the power of death, that is, the devil. (emphasis mine)

The key word here is "had"—he doesn't anymore!

We also see in the Gospel of Luke that Jesus fasted for forty days, during which Satan came to him with various temptations. Let's look specifically at Luke 4:5–8:

> [5] Then the devil, taking Him up on a high mountain,

showed Him all the kingdoms of the world in a moment of time. [6] And the devil said to Him, *"All this authority I will give You, and their glory; for this has been delivered to me, and I give it to whomever I wish. [7] Therefore, if You will worship before me, all will be Yours."* (emphasis mine)

[8] And Jesus answered and said to him, "Get behind Me, Satan! For it is written, 'You shall worship the Lord your God, and Him only you shall serve.'"

We're about to get into it here, but understanding this point is important to gaining victory in every area of life.

The entire earth was given to Satan by Adam and Eve—not sold for a discount, not bartered, but *given* away. This allowed Satan to set up a system counter to the Kingdom of God. Satan had the power to set up and promote anyone who was willing to bow down to his way of doing things. Satan also controlled all sectors of civilization: government, entertainment, law, business, religion, finance, family, and so on. Things got so bad that in Genesis 6, a flood came and destroyed all of humanity except for Noah and his family (a total of eight people). Let that sink in for a moment.

In Luke 4, when Jesus was tempted, notice that Satan said that the kingdoms were "delivered" to him, and he had the power to give them to whomever he wanted. If this were not a legitimate temptation, it would not have been mentioned in scriptures. Before the death, burial, and resurrection of Jesus, these claims by Satan were legal and binding in the courts of heaven. But after Jesus' resurrection and assumption of his position at the right hand of God the Father, Satan became a squatter. All a squatter needs to do to lay claim to a property is to establish residence, as proved by a piece of mail or utility bill or something similar. In the case of Satan, all he has left to establish a fake form of control of the earth is the mouth of mankind: "For by your words you will be justified, and by your words you will be condemned" (Matthew 12:37).

Words (I should say *wrong* words) give Satan legal authority to bring to pass that which we really do not want. Look at Job 6:24–25:

> 24 "Teach me, and I will hold my tongue;
> Cause me to understand wherein I have erred.
> 25 How forceful are right words!"

Words have power. Even though Satan had his power knocked down by Jesus, humankind ignorantly continues to give him power, as we are speaking spirits—that is, since God is a spirit and humanity is made in the image of God, we are spirit, have a soul, and live in a physical body that allows us to speak. Every time we violate the commandments of the Most High, we allow Satan to continue to squat in our homes, our businesses, and our lives.

Deception is the only other tool Satan has to use in

our lives. We need the wisdom of the Most High to get above Satan's world system. Old habits with Satan die hard, but die they must. Let's prove that while Satan may be the god of this world system, he is not the god of the earth. He is nothing more than a squatter.

True freedom is the freedom of *choice*. To choose life or death, blessing or curse, revelation or information, proper management or mismanagement. It's a hard lesson but an empowering one as well, because now our decisions can be intentional. As you know, the Son of God came to reverse the disaster of the Fall and to give humanity another opportunity to repent and accept the finished work of Jesus Christ in order to dominate this life as was originally intended.

I want to say again: *The Most High has dealt with humanity differently than any other creature ever made, as we have been given the power of choice.*

## THE PROJECT PERSPECTIVE

Whew. That was a lot of biblical analysis. You may be wondering how to apply these teachings more directly to your life. Never fear. While each chapter starts with the biblical perspective, you'll always get a more practical, actionable take as well. So, let's look at the project charter.

In project management, the *project charter* is the document (or process) that formally authorizes the existence of a project and gives the project manager the authority to apply organizational resources to project activities. Just as the original charter for humanity defined our collective purpose of stewardship, the project charter defines the project purpose. It typically identifies team members, deliverables, a timeline, budget and other resources, and success criteria. Because organizations have limited resources, we must be good managers and stewards of what we are given to work with. Nothing belongs to us—we are taking care of it on behalf of the organization (which in a broad sense is the Kingdom of God). Failure to manage properly leads to a loss of resources and outcomes that are contrary to the original vision.

When I worked at an engineering firm in downtown Chicago, the principal (the CEO of the firm) was adamant that every engineering project have a project charter. While we referred to it as a project management plan, it was essentially a charter (just be aware you may hear charters called different names). It was a good rule, because we discovered that when a solid plan was not in place, our projects faced major issues: blown budgets, late schedules, conflicts within the team, lack of quality control—all of which eventually led to angry clients and lost revenue. These kinds of issues, if not immediately corrected, can end a business altogether.

As a project manager, I hated making these plans— the process can be tedious, and the plan must be constantly updated. I was also required to have periodic team meetings to share the plan and to hold team members accountable for complying with it. In the end, not only was the charter a great reference to monitor the project until completion, but it also provided real metrics to measure the success or failure of the project.

You can apply the project charter concept to your personal life as well—defining your purpose, your goals, and the resources you have available. Every human being has a unique gift or talent that starts as a seed and must be nourished and grown. Do you understand your gifts and how they support your purpose?

## REFLECTION QUESTIONS

+ What is your purpose and your sphere of influence?
+ Have you been faithful in your realm of responsibility?
+ How do you see yourself as a manager or steward in your professional life? Your personal life?
+ Have you been diligent and consistent in bringing your talents and gifts to the forefront?
+ In what areas would you like to exercise greater stewardship or management?

# Principle 2: Stewardship

*The purpose of management is stewardship.*
*Whether we are working with the earth,*
*a business, or our family, we have limited*
*resources; we must use them wisely.*

## THE BIBLICAL PERSPECTIVE

We spoke in the last chapter about the idea of the world system—the one that relies on logic, reason, and the senses—versus the Kingdom system, the heaven-on-earth that was widely available to humankind before the Fall. Since the Fall, God has been trying to reestablish his kingdom here on earth, and our job is to help. In this chapter, we'll discuss some principles (mechanics) of how the Kingdom of God works and what our responsibilities are in managing and growing what we've been given.

Let's start with the premise that the Most High expects the earth to be a copy of heaven in every way, with an abundance of resources and no poverty. That world existed before and it can exist again. Several principles come from that premise.

**The King owns everything.** The wealth of the Kingdom is the sole property of the King. The wealth and resources on this planet do not belong to us but rather to him. Humanity simply has the privilege of using these resources for our benefit and to accomplish *his* purposes (see Deuteronomy 8:17–18).

**We own nothing.** The flip side of the prior point is that if God owns everything, we own nothing. We are simply stewarding the earth. So the idea of independence—the ideology of personal ownership—is anti-Kingdom. (Just let that sink in for a bit.)

**Kingdom management is a gift.** The Most High God has gifted humanity the task of managing his affairs with excellence, efficiency, and profitability.

**Our task is to grow resources.** Our job is to take care of the earth and its resources and to be productive in its care and maintenance. We are also tasked with multiplying and advancing anything that is given to us within our sphere of influence. But to do so, we must work not for money but rather for purpose. When we work for purpose, wealth will come in abundance.

**Riches come from God.** The Lord God gives us the power to obtain wealth so that *he*—not we—may establish his kingdom here on this earth (Deuteronomy 8:18). I Timothy 6:17–19 helps us understand how to handle riches for the Kingdom:

> [17] Command those who are rich in this present age not to be haughty, nor to trust in uncertain riches but in the living God, who gives us richly all things to enjoy. [18] Let them do good, that they be rich in good works, ready to give, willing to share, [19] storing up for themselves a good foundation for the time to come, that they may lay hold on eternal life.

Simple but profound. There are no excuses for not being rich the correct way.

**We are accountable and responsible.** Resources are entrusted to the kingdom citizen, and the kingdom citizen is responsible and accountable to the King for the use and management of his resources. Faithfulness equals accountability, and the kingdom citizen will be required to give an account as to what was done with the resources. "For by your words you will be justified, and by your words you will be condemned" (Matthew 12:37).

**What you mismanage you will lose.** Scarcity and poverty are not God's fault. They come from a lack of productivity through mismanagement of resources, which is a direct result of laziness and wickedness. "The rich man's wealth is his strong city; the destruction of the poor is their poverty" (Proverbs 10:15). Whatever you mismanage, you will eventually lose. To prosper, we must get rid of the scarcity mentality. "For as [a man] thinks in his heart, so is he" (Proverbs 23:7).

There are many more tenets that could be included here, but these are just a few relating to stewardship. *It is an honor and a great responsibility to have a life on this planet—and the Most High God is expecting a return on his investment.*

To explore this concept further, let's look at one of the most famous parables about stewardship, the parable of the talents, which is found in Matthew 25:14–30. (In biblical times, a *talent* was a unit of measure for precious metals.)

[14] "For the kingdom of heaven is like a man traveling to a far country, who called his own servants and delivered his goods to them. [15] And to one he gave five talents, to another two, and to another one, to each according to his own ability; and immediately he went on a journey. [16] Then he who had received the five talents went and traded with them, and made another five talents. [17] And likewise he who had received two gained two more also. [18] But he who had received one went and dug in the ground, and hid his lord's money. [19] After a long time the lord of those servants came and settled accounts with them.

[20] "So he who had received five talents came and brought five other talents, saying, 'Lord, you delivered

to me five talents; look, I have gained five more talents besides them.' <sup>21</sup> His lord said to him, 'Well done, good and faithful servant; you were faithful over a few things, I will make you ruler over many things. Enter into the joy of your lord.' <sup>22</sup> He also who had received two talents came and said, 'Lord, you delivered to me two talents; look, I have gained two more talents besides them.' <sup>23</sup> His lord said to him, 'Well done, good and faithful servant; you have been faithful over a few things, I will make you ruler over many things. Enter into the joy of your lord.'

<sup>24</sup> "Then he who had received the one talent came and said, 'Lord, I knew you to be a hard man, reaping where you have not sown, and gathering where you have not scattered seed. <sup>25</sup> And I was afraid, and went and hid your talent in the ground. Look, there you have what is yours.'

<sup>26</sup> "But his lord answered and said to him, 'You wicked and lazy servant, you knew that I reap where I have not sown, and gather where I have not scattered seed. <sup>27</sup> So you ought to have deposited my money with the bankers, and at my coming I would have received back my own with interest. <sup>28</sup> So take the talent from him, and give it to him who has ten talents.

<sup>29</sup> 'For to everyone who has, more will be given, and he will have abundance; but from him who does not have, even what he has will be taken away. <sup>30</sup> And cast the unprofitable servant into the outer darkness. There will be weeping and gnashing of teeth.'

What I truly love about the idea of biblical mechanics is the idea that real-life examples are given to express a hidden profound truth. Once again, let's look at this both from a practical (project management) standpoint and of course from a spiritual perspective.

A project charter was given to these three individuals, each according to their abilities: steward this money. Also, for you religious folks who hate talking about money, in biblical times, as I mentioned above, a *talent* was a unit of measure for precious metals. So, while we can certainly interpret "talent" as skill or gift (and we should), in this story, we are clearly speaking about currency. (Believe it or not, Jesus spoke about money and stewardship more than he did about the second coming.)

Every person who has ever lived on this planet has had a talent or gift that nobody else possesses. It is unique to that person. The master dealt wisely and gave much thought before distributing the management of his business.

The master went away for a long time, but part of the definition of a project is that eventually it has a termination date—the master will eventually come back. No instruction was given the managers as to how to proceed; it was left to them to use their own particular styles to complete the project successfully.

The Most High has records (or "metrics," in project speak) that he will use to judge us as kingdom citizens. For example, in I Corinthians 3:12–15 we read:

[12] Now if anyone builds on this foundation with gold, silver, precious stones, wood, hay, straw, [13] each one's work will become clear; for the day will declare it, because it will be revealed by fire; and the fire will test each one's work, of what sort it is. [14] If anyone's work which he has built on it endures, he will receive a reward. [15] If anyone's work is burned, he will suffer loss; but he himself will be saved, yet so as through fire.

We must judge if the assigned project or task was successful or not, and if not, then why not. There are no shortcuts in getting the assignment completed. Everything will be scrutinized for the proper results and outcomes.

The Most High rewards diligence and productivity. Poverty is a direct result of lack of productivity. The rewards given are always of greater measure than the efforts required to complete various tasks for the Kingdom of God.

Now, let's get to this "wicked and lazy" servant. This dude came out of the gate in entirely the wrong headspace, so he gets nothing but the riot act read to him. This guy was not at all profitable. He had the same opportunities as the other two managers, yet he didn't want to use his abilities to prosper the investment. Where were the meetings, collaboration, or strategy? We know that 80 to 90 percent of a project manager's task is simple communication, but this guy did not communicate with anyone!

It appears he was fearful, which can be paralyzing and can keep an individual from thinking clearly. But as II Timothy 1:7 says, "For God has not given us a spirit of fear, but of power and of love and of a sound mind."

Additionally, this manager had the same opportunities as the other two, but rather than taking responsibility for his inaction, he decided to speak about how wicked his boss was (the one who gave him the opportunity in the first place). His response was downright disrespectful. Again, I remind you of Matthew 12:37: "For by your words you will be justified, and by your words you will be condemned." Contrary to popular opinion, you can't just let anything come out of your mouth (I'm sure for some of y'all that comes as a shock). This wicked and lazy servant spoke of his own demise in his response to the owner. He condemned himself by his words and his belief system: "For as [a man] thinks in his heart, so is he" (Proverbs 23:7).

Let me emphasize what I think is a key point in this parable: *The Most High God will not give you more than you can manage.* Just as the master in this story assessed who could manage what, God assesses how much you can handle. So stop praying and asking for more money and responsibility if you haven't managed well what you already have!

There are consequences for mismanaging God's resources, which, to be clear, include things like your finances, your marriage, and your health. In this case, this servant was fired on the spot, put out of the stewardship position. When we fail in our stewardship, our stance should be to repent, do some introspection as to where we went wrong, and then correct the deficiency immediately and not be arrogant in our ignorance. (I always say that it's one thing to be wrong, but quite another to be loud and wrong!)

Let's look again at Matthew 25:29:

'For to everyone who has, more will be given, and he will have abundance; but from him who does not have, even what he has will be taken away.'

It appears that the saying "the rich get richer and the poor get poorer" came directly from Jesus himself! Now wait a minute, that's pretty harsh. However, there is a critical principle here. The Most High frowns on slothfulness and lack of productivity. James 1:5 says (I paraphrase) that if you lack wisdom, you need to ask it of God and he will give it. God has made a heavy investment in each and every one of us to complete our assignment upon this earth, and we all need to take that assignment seriously indeed.


## THE PROJECT PERSPECTIVE

Let's put some of this into more practical terms.

As a manager or leader, the responsibility for success or failure starts and ends with you. A manager must make a clear assessment of available resources, personnel, and objectives. And they must manage scope, schedule, costs, risk, quality assurance, and so on. A leader must go a step further and learn to see the larger picture, as this is where we move well beyond implementation and into communication and creativity.

One of the first things I recommend for successful stewardship of a project is collaboration in the form of meetings and group discussion. There is safety in "a multitude of counsel," and your team is your responsibility. Any new vision or changes that you desire need to be clearly communicated to your team and implemented in increments. (I'll speak about that concept further when we discuss change management.) Also, as a leader, it's important to recognize that you don't know everything. It's okay—more than okay actually—to do your due diligence and research as well as to speak with subject matter experts. In the parable, the one-talent guy failed to collaborate and to do everything he could to get the information he needed to be successful, and he was left with nothing.

But our stewardship is not just in business—a "project" could include family or community projects as well as business projects. I myself can offer an example of what failure on a personal project looks like . . .

I was married for fourteen years to a family practice physician. We had different backgrounds, but we loved our differences, at least at first. I came from a stable two-parent household on the far south side of Chicago;

unfortunately, my wife's dad had died young, and she became the leader for her mom and sister. When we got married, I thought we would be together forever. However, we must steward what we are given for it to flourish.

We were two professionals with two boys living in a nice suburb, and folks knew us well. Unfortunately, due to our upbringing and socialization, we deemed different things to be important. For me, if things seemed smooth in the relationship, I didn't worry about it and felt no need to talk about it. I certainly had tunnel vision, as I was busy with my career and trying to be a good husband and father. I've always been an automatic-cruise-control individual.

By contrast, my wife was more expressive in her communication style. She was constantly talking and always wanted to know details of everything. Well, talking was not my strong suit, and I was resistant to change. The way I was raised, it was assumed you would go to school, be a good citizen, and so on. We didn't talk about things; we just executed. But not everyone is like that. Some people like to be reassured that they are loved or beautiful or valued. For me, verbal expression was a weak point. (It's not just a stereotype that engineers sometimes tend to be too focused on tasks.) In my case, I didn't see the negative factors that were building in our marriage: my wife and I didn't go on regular dates, we didn't communicate regularly, we didn't check to make sure that our goals were aligned.

As a result of our ongoing misalignment in communication and expectations, we ended up divorced. For a long time, I was at a loss. What was the disconnect?

I am happy to report that (with some personal reflection and growth) we are still cordial to this day, and we have two great boys who have grown up well despite the situation. But if we had both been more engaged and aligned in stewarding our relationship, things might have been different.

Nevertheless, I want to return to the Adam and Eve story to further illustrate my point. I personally believe that everyone involved in any assignment, no matter how big or small, must be fully committed to it. Adam and Eve were *both* given the mandate by the Most High to not eat the fruit of the tree of the knowledge of good and evil. But Adam was busy taking care of Kingdom business, while Eve was having a full-blown conversation with a serpent. Ultimately, they *both* failed to keep their end of the bargain—as did my wife and I in managing our marriage.

Leaders must be watchful and attentive all the time. When a task or project fails to meet objectives, the leader must be ready to do an overall assessment. In other words, when we fail to follow the doctrines and guidelines as laid out by the Most High—when we fail to manage our project or our marriage—failure of the entire effort is at some point inevitable.

## REFLECTION QUESTIONS

+ What "projects" do you manage?
+ How do you steward those projects and apply the management and leadership lessons we've discussed so far?
+ Have you ever failed when given the opportunity of leadership? Reflecting on this chapter, what insights about that failure do you have?
+ On what projects could you have done better? Which tools could have made a difference?
+ Where have you succeeded in stewarding your life and your projects?

# PRINCIPLE 3: A SOLID FOUNDATION

*We must build on a solid foundation.*
*If we do not, whatever we build—*
*a project, a house, a life—can crumble away*
*due to a relatively small "storm."*

## THE BIBLICAL PERSPECTIVE

There are no shortcuts to building a strong foundation. Talent without process and principles will get you success but not "good success" (Joshua 1:8). This principle is key in leadership. We cannot assume that our technical expertise in any given field automatically qualifies us for leadership. Technical and leadership skills are different, and if you're not careful, you will get exposed for your lack of the needed foundation. When all is said and done, how successful was your business? Your family and relationships? Your health and finances? We ultimately are judged on results and outcomes.

Let's look at a scripture that deals with this issue. In Matthew 7:24–27, Jesus speaks in a parable:

24 "Therefore whoever hears these sayings of Mine, and does them, I will liken him to a wise man who built his house on the rock: 25 and the rain descended, the floods came, and the winds blew and beat on that house; and it did not fall, for it was founded on the rock.

26 "But everyone who hears these sayings of Mine, and does not do them, will be like a foolish man who built his house on the sand: 27 and the rain descended, the floods came, and the winds blew and beat on that house; and it fell. And great was its fall."

Let's unpack this one (it's about to get deep—again!). Both of the houses mentioned were built on what appeared to be firm foundations, and under normal circumstances, there was no distinction between them. This is where the Enemy locks in. We don't know the strength of the soils holding these foundations in place until a stress factor is applied. Notice, the stress factors (the rain, floods, and wind) hit *both* houses—the weather doesn't distinguish between a wise man and a foolish man.

When the elements hit the house of the foolish man,

it was a total disaster, causing not only loss but likely also embarrassment. How could something that looks so stable on the outside be so shaky and unstable inside? This is what happens when humankind relies on sense, knowledge, facts, and education as opposed to the truths of the Most High God. Natural knowledge will get us only to a certain point, and then failure, frustration, and loss are inevitable. However, when we rely on the word of God for our wisdom and knowledge, when (not if) the rains, floods, and wind come, our foundation will hold in place and not waver or move.

The issues and problems that humanity faces in the first quarter of the twenty-first century will not be solved in the natural realm but will require access to the wisdom of the Most High in order for us to stand and not be moved.

## THE PROJECT PERSPECTIVE

A literal example of this principle was displayed in its fullness when I was a sophomore at Northwestern University McCormick School of Engineering and Applied Science.

As part of our basic civil engineering curriculum, we had a class called Soil Mechanics. One day during our lab time, the professor did an experiment with a square tank filled with fine compressed sand. He placed a small circular weight on top of the soil, and the soil appeared to hold the weight in place. We were astonished to see the weight just sit there looking stable on the surface.

Then, he took a cylindrical metal pipe and struck the side of the tank. Down that weight went! It sank so fast that it looked like a magic trick!

The next thing the professor said has stuck with me to this day: "Always make sure your soils are tested for stress and compaction to be able to support the weight of any given foundation. The soils must hold up to bearing pressures and all sorts of stress."

## REFLECTION QUESTIONS

+ When have you relied on your own knowledge and intelligence to solve an issue, only to find out that you were missing key elements—things that never even occurred to you?
+ When addressing a situation, are you more concerned with symbolism or substance?
+ How can you be more diligent and consistent in dedicating yourself to the process and not just to the expected outcomes?
+ When have you succeeded in building a firm foundation that withstood a strong "storm"?

# PRINCIPLE 4: ACCOUNTABILITY

*We are accountable for our actions and inactions. Integrity is an essential virtue. A lack of integrity can destroy our efforts, projects, and life.*

## THE BIBLICAL PERSPECTIVE

One example that shows a lack of management skills and accountability can be found in Luke 16:1–13, the parable of the unjust steward:

[1] He also said to His disciples: "There was a certain rich man who had a steward, and an accusation was brought to him that this man was wasting his goods.

[2] So he called him and said to him, 'What is this I hear about you? Give an account of your stewardship, for you can no longer be steward.'

[3] "Then the steward said within himself, 'What shall I do? For my master is taking the stewardship away from me. I cannot dig; I am ashamed to beg. [4] I have resolved what to do, that when I am put out of the stewardship, they may receive me into their houses.'

[5] "So he called every one of his master's debtors to him, and said to the first, 'How much do you owe my master?' [6] And he said, 'A hundred measures of oil.' So he said to him, 'Take your bill, and sit down quickly and write fifty.' [7] Then he said to another, 'And how much do you owe?' So he said, 'A hundred measures of wheat.' And he said to him, 'Take your bill, and write eighty.' [8] So the master commended the unjust steward because he had dealt shrewdly. For the sons of this world are more shrewd in their generation than the sons of light.

[9] "And I say to you, make friends for yourselves by unrighteous mammon, that when you fail, they may receive you into an everlasting home. [10] He who is faithful in what is least is faithful also in much; and he who is unjust in what is least is unjust also in much. [11] Therefore if you have not been faithful in the unrighteous mammon, who will commit to your trust the true riches? [12] And if you have not been faithful in what is another man's, who will give you what is your own?

[13] "No servant can serve two masters; for either he will hate the one and love the other, or else he will be loyal to the one and despise the other. You cannot serve God and mammon."

Looks like we have another wicked and lazy servant (seems to be a recurring theme). This dude is even more scandalous than the one-talent guy in the parable of the talents.

When we hear about a "certain rich man," we understand that this man was well known in the community and had a thriving business. He was also *not* in the habit of having a bunch of trifling staff working for him. He must have been embarrassed when word came back that his steward was wasting his goods. We really are not told how they were being wasted, but certainly it was not a good thing. In any organization, few things are more important than project management, and when that is screwed up, it can be catastrophic to the entire organization, potentially to the point of full business collapse.

This manager was definitely capable of managing properly, and yet he didn't. I want you to stop and really think about this point. There are *no* shortcuts. We know this because typically you don't get rich in any kind of business venture without having great staff and managers around you. I've learned personally that having a strong team to call on for assistance is not only efficient, but it also leaves you in a position to gain even more wealth and business through the art of delegation. For instance, for me, everyone from my barber, cleaning crew, and CPA to my property managers, landscapers, and attorneys has aided me tremendously in being more efficient with my time. My point is that this particular manager was not just someone off the street; he was there to get the job done, and to do it well and gain more profits. What's tragic about this story is that the rich man (owner) "heard" of the foolishness from someone else. The rich man didn't have time to micro-manage this guy, so to hear about misappropriation of funds had to be infuriating, to say the least.

When the jig was up, instead of confessing to the owner, this lazy manager started to scheme to cut a break with the owner's debtors. We don't know if the owner knew of the manager giving discounts to his debtors, but the manager was "commended" for his actions. Here's where it gets interesting, and Jesus starts to do some serious teaching on this subject. In verse 8, we read that "the sons of this world are more shrewd in their generation than the sons of light"! I don't know about you, but as a believer in the Almighty God and follower of Christ himself, that statement got me hot under the collar. This dude came up with a scheme to not only save his backside with his owner, but he also made friends with his owner's debtors so that if he were to end up getting fired, he would have a soft landing elsewhere. I want to reiterate (again) that there is a difference between the Children of This World and the

Children of Light. The former use their flesh, feelings, and this world system to survive, and the Children of Light are supposed to use Kingdom principles of diligence, wisdom, honesty, and transparency to thrive. The way things appear, the Children of This World look smarter and wiser because they have all but mastered the system that will eventually be judged as counterfeit and fraud (just go back to the example of the foundation of quicksand).

Once again, God will not give you more than you are able to manage well. Verse 10 tells us that those who are faithful in the small things will be faithful in the bigger things; if you can't manage the small, you can't manage the big. And verse 11 tells us that if we can't steward another's goods, it's unlikely we can steward our own. This verse also establishes that money and material things are the least in the Kingdom of God—true riches are the anointing and empowerment to prosper. If you do well in stewarding the small and large things and understand the true riches, excellent. However, if you have mismanaged parts of your life and wasted opportunities the Most High has given you freely, don't try to cover up your malfeasance. Repent for being a bad manager and then ask to be put back into stewardship.

In case it's not already clear, a key element to being a good steward is *integrity*, which we've defined as the essential quality of being honest, having strong moral principles, and staying true to those values and beliefs, even when it's unpopular or inconvenient.

Integrity sometimes seems like a rare quality in today's world, where dishonesty and deceit are so prevalent. It's easy to fall into the trap of compromising our values for personal gain or recognition, and even if you have worked diligently to reach a certain level of success in life, a lapse in judgment can destroy everything.

As believers and followers of Christ, we're called to live a life of integrity, to align our actions with our beliefs. The Bible provides us with numerous examples of men and women who demonstrated unwavering integrity in the face of adversity. By examining their lives, we can learn how to live with integrity.

**Joseph** is one of the most well-known examples of integrity in the Bible (see Genesis 39–41). He was sold into slavery by his own brothers and later imprisoned after being falsely accused of sexual assault. Despite these trials, Joseph remained faithful to God and maintained his integrity. He refused to compromise his beliefs or take advantage of his position as Potiphar's servant. He even resisted the advances of Potiphar's wife, which would have been an easy path to gain favor and avoid punishment. In the end, God elevated Joseph to a position of power in Egypt, fulfilling the dreams he had received as a young man.

When Joseph reached the rank of prime minister (second only to Pharaoh himself), he had to hold to his integrity of forgiveness and not try to exact revenge against his brothers for selling him into slavery. Jesus said in Mark 11: 25–26:

[25] "And whenever you stand praying, if you have anything against anyone, forgive him, that your Father in heaven may also forgive you your trespasses. [26] But if you do not forgive, neither will your Father in heaven forgive your trespasses."

Joseph had the power to have his brothers put to death for what they did, but instead treated them like royalty and saved their lives during the great famine.

Joseph's story teaches us that integrity is not just about doing what is right, but also about maintaining our moral principles in the face of temptation and adversity. Joseph could have easily compromised his beliefs and taken advantage of his position, but he chose to remain faithful to God and honor his values. This unwavering commitment to integrity ultimately led to his success and favor with God.

**Job** is another biblical character who exemplifies integrity (see Job 1–42). He was a wealthy man who lost everything he had, including his family, possessions, and health. Despite these trials, Job remained faithful to God and refused to curse him or blame him for his misfortunes. He acknowledged that God was sovereign and just, even though he didn't understand why he was suffering. In the end, God restored Job's fortunes and blessed him with even greater wealth than before.

Job's story teaches us that integrity is not just about doing what is right when things are going well, but also about maintaining our faith and trust in God when we face difficulties and trials. Job's faithfulness in the face of adversity ultimately led to his restoration and blessing from God.

**Daniel** was a young man who was taken captive by the Babylonians and brought to serve in King Nebuchadnezzar's palace. Despite the temptation to conform to Babylonian culture, Daniel remained faithful to God and refused to eat the king's food or drink his wine, which would have violated Jewish dietary laws. He also refused to bow down to the king's statue, even when threatened with death. As a result, God protected Daniel and his friends, and they were able to prosper in Babylon (see Daniel 1–6).

Daniel's story teaches us that integrity is not just about doing what is right for ourselves, but also about standing up for what is right in the eyes of God, even when it's not popular or convenient. Daniel's faithfulness to God ultimately led to his protection and prosperity, despite the challenges he faced.

**Ruth** is a biblical character who demonstrated integrity through her loyalty and faithfulness. A Moabite woman, she married into an Israelite family. When her husband died, she refused to abandon her mother-in-law, Naomi, and returned with her to Israel. Despite the challenges of being a foreigner in a new land, Ruth remained faithful to God and to Naomi. She worked hard in the fields to provide for them and even married Boaz, a close relative of Naomi, in accordance with Jewish customs. Ruth gave birth to a son, whose own grandson would become King David; ultimately, Ruth would be included in the lineage of Jesus (see Ruth 1–4).

Ruth's story teaches us that integrity is not just about doing what is right for ourselves or God, but also about showing loyalty and faithfulness to those around us. Ruth's commitment to Naomi and her willingness to work hard and sacrifice for her led to her blessing and favor with God.

**Jesus** is the ultimate example of integrity, living a sinless life and always doing what was right in the eyes of God. He never wavered in his commitment to God's will, even when faced with intense persecution and suffering. He taught his disciples to love their enemies, forgive those who wronged them, and show compassion to the poor and needy. Jesus ultimately demonstrated his integrity by sacrificing himself on the cross for the forgiveness of sins, fulfilling God's plan for the salvation of humanity (Matthew 26–28, John 3:16).

Jesus' life and lessons teach us that integrity is not just about doing what is right, but also about loving and serving others. Jesus' commitment to God's will and his selfless sacrifice on the cross demonstrated his unwavering integrity and love for humanity.

Need more biblical references about integrity? Try these:

The integrity of the upright will guide them, but the perversity of the unfaithful will destroy them. (Proverbs 11:3)

Better is the poor who walks in his integrity than one perverse in his ways, though he be rich. (Proverbs 28:6)

Having a good conscience, that when they defame you as evildoers, those who revile your good conduct in Christ may be ashamed. (I Peter 3:16)

Lying lips are an abomination to the Lord, but those who deal truthfully are His delight. (Proverbs 12:22)

To do righteousness and justice *is* more acceptable to the Lord than sacrifice. (Proverbs 21:3)

Providing honorable things, not only in the sight of the Lord, but also in the sight of men. (2 Corinthians 8:21)

[11] By this I know that You are well pleased with me, because my enemy does not triumph over me. [12] As for me, You uphold me in my integrity, and set me before Your face forever. (Psalm 41:11–12)

Pray for us; for we are confident that we have a good conscience, in all things desiring to live honorably. (Hebrews 13:18)

The way of the just is uprightness; O Most Upright, You weigh the path of the just. (Isaiah 26:7)

[1] In the meantime, when an innumerable multitude of people had gathered together, so that they trampled one another, He began to say to His disciples first of all, beware of the leaven of the Pharisees, which is hypocrisy. [2] For there is nothing covered that will not be revealed, nor hidden that will not be known. [3] Therefore whatever you have spoken in the dark will be heard in the light, and what you have spoken in the ear in inner rooms will be proclaimed on the housetops. (Luke 12:1–3)

Of all the scriptures I have mentioned, I especially want to point out Psalm 41:11–12. Integrity will not only win you favor, but it will also stop your enemies in their tracks. It provides you with a level of protection that you most certainly need dealing with this demonic cesspool called "Earth."

## THE PROJECT PERSPECTIVE

Lack of integrity can take many forms on a project team: team members not completing tasks correctly or not completing them in a timely manner, team members not communicating proactively, a project manager not clearly explaining contingences to the executive team. These types of things can throw the project schedule off track, cause risk and quality issues, or simply generate ill will.

On a project team, problems and issues need to be addressed as early as possible, and regularly throughout the course of a project. The more a project is behind schedule or over budget, the harder it is to get things back on track. The project team must be transparent in discussing where things went wrong, take responsibility for missteps, and then be part of the solution. Not being honest and placing blame on others are examples of integrity breaches. Some tools that can help with communication and transparency include project plans, status reports, team meetings, and metrics that track progress with hard data in real time.

The following story is a perfect example of what I'm talking about when it comes to integrity in project management.

After college graduation, my first full-time assignment was with the Illinois Department of Transportation (known as IDOT), where I entered a three-year rotation program for entry-level civil engineers. I was assigned to a roadway reconstruction project with multiple tasks: drainage, traffic signals, concrete, asphalt work. One Friday afternoon, I was finishing up some inspection work on a storm sewer pipe when the contractor ran out of the crushed stone and trench backfill material that holds the pipe in place.

Instead of calling the plant to get a late load shipped out, it was suggested that we just use the excavated material to cover the rest of the pipe run. The contractor obviously didn't want to pay for the needed extra material, but this approach would be a clear violation of the standard specifications, and could cause the pipe to shift over time and eventually break.

I told the crew chief absolutely not, that this material was required per the contract. This individual proceeded to pull out a large roll of $100 bills and suggested that I start my weekend early—wink, wink, nudge, nudge. I must admit, it was quite a roll of Benjamins! What would be the harm? There was only a short stretch of pipe left.

Well, thank goodness I let that thought go, as I didn't want anyone to come back and accuse me of taking a bribe and then have my career go bust before it even got started. I once heard one of my cousins say, "Whatever you compromise to get, you'll have to compromise to keep." I therefore told the crew chief that he had exactly five seconds to put that wad back in his pocket, and then to come back on Monday, act like he had some sense, and finish the project accordingly.

Let's be clear, it was a nice hunk of change I turned down, and nobody would have been the wiser, but as I've mentioned, Satan is the god of this world system and his job is to establish conditions that deceive humankind into buckling under what I call "downward pressure." Keep in mind also that the act of compromise can always, and most likely will, come back to you in the future, usually at a time that is most inconvenient: "Do not be deceived, God is not mocked; for whatever a man sows, that he will also reap" (Galatians 6:7). We've heard everyone from preachers and politicians to lawyers and entertainers reaping the results of sowing "bad seeds." It's interesting that the Most High uses the term "mocked," which suggests making something seem laughable, unreal, or impossible, or to treat with contempt or disdain. I assure you that the principle of integrity, among all the others, is critical to follow to the letter, as it applies to both positive and negative situations in life.

## REFLECTION QUESTIONS

+ In what ways has integrity (or lack thereof) affected your life and outcomes?
+ When you did not act with integrity, how could you have operated differently?
+ What boundaries could you establish for yourself that will help keep you from violating this principle?
+ Can you think of situations that could immediately improve or benefit from direct application of this principle?
+ When have you succeeded in acting with integrity in a challenging situation?

# PRINCIPLE 5: DELEGATION

*Delegation expands our capacity.*
*A good steward uses delegation to*
*get more done and to develop others*
*but remains engaged.*

## THE BIBLICAL PERSPECTIVE

In Exodus 18:13–27, the children of Israel and Moses, their leader, have been delivered out of the hands of Pharaoh of Egypt after 430 years of slavery and bondage, and are now in the wilderness preparing to go into the land of Canaan. During this time, Moses is counseling close to three million folks on the laws and precepts of God. His father-in-law, Jethro, comes and tries to talk some sense into Moses about his sloppy management skills. We read as follows:

[13] And so it was, on the next day, that Moses sat to judge the people; and the people stood before Moses from morning until evening. [14] So when Moses' father-in-law saw all that he did for the people, he said, "What is this thing that you are doing for the people? Why do you alone sit, and all the people stand before you from morning until evening?"

[15] And Moses said to his father-in-law, "Because the people come to me to inquire of God. [16] When they have a difficulty, they come to me, and I judge between one and another; and I make known the statutes of God and His laws."

[17] So Moses' father-in-law said to him, "The thing that you do is not good. [18] Both you and these people who are with you will surely wear yourselves out. For this thing is too much for you; you are not able to perform it by yourself. [19] Listen now to my voice; I will give you counsel, and God will be with you: Stand before God for the people, so that you may bring the difficulties to God. [20] And you shall teach them the statutes and the laws, and show them the way in which they must walk and the work they must do. [21] Moreover you shall select from all the people able men, such as fear God, men of truth, hating covetousness; and place such over them to be rulers of thousands, rulers of hundreds, rulers of fifties, and rulers of tens.

[22] And let them judge the people at all times. Then it will be that every great matter they shall bring to you, but every small matter they themselves shall judge. So it will be easier for you, for they will bear the burden with you. [23] If you do this thing, and God so commands you, then you will be able to endure, and all this people will also go to their place in peace."

[24] So Moses heeded the voice of his father-in-law and did all that he had said. [25] And Moses chose able men out of all Israel, and made them heads over the people: rulers of thousands, rulers of hundreds, rulers of fifties, and rulers of tens. [26] So they judged the people at all times; the hard cases they brought to Moses, but they judged every small case themselves.

[27] Then Moses let his father-in-law depart, and he went his way to his own land.

In other words, Moses needed to learn to delegate! Notice a few things about this story: Moses was trying to do everything himself, and his father-in-law rightly observed that this would lead to burnout. But his father-in-law didn't say "just leave them to their own devices." Rather, he told Moses to choose qualified people to become leaders under him, to educate them properly, and then to let them handle the smaller day-to-day decisions but to bring larger decisions to him. (So Jethro was a pretty good business coach!) Moses had to stay engaged to make sure the delegated tasks were done effectively.

But the benefit of Moses' delegation was much greater than just avoiding burnout. By letting others "share the burden," collectively they could accomplish much more. Imagine the queue if Moses had continued to do everything himself! Luckily, even though Moses was the leader designated by God to make whatever decisions were required, he was wise enough to not get offended by his father-in-law's unsolicited advice.

## THE PROJECT PERSPECTIVE

In project management (remember your "project" can be in your personal life as well as work life), the art of delegation is critical. If not clearly thought out and well executed, it can jeopardize the project and lead to failure. Delegation is not abdication; the project manager must remain engaged even when delegating.

I see three keys to successful delegation:
+ Understanding whom to delegate to.
+ Communicating clearly and regularly.
+ Trusting staff to do the work, while still being available for them.

**Staffing.** Every manager is responsible for the staff and resources under their authority. A manager must look at things from a 40,000-foot view and be creative yet practical. By accurately assessing their team members' strengths and weaknesses, the manager can identify who is a good fit to perform each task. In some cases, you may need to assign the best of the best; for instance, on a highly critical task with no wiggle room in the project plan, you might want your most expert team member. In many cases though, delegation is an opportunity to develop your staff by giving them new challenges that stretch their skills or expose them to a new area of the business. In short, delegation is a tool for team development.

**Communication.** I like to think of staff as extensions of the project manager or leader (I call it the "octopus principle"). Although others carry out the tasks, the spirit of the execution should come from the manager or leader. This means clear communication of the project charter, vision, and objectives, as well as the specific objectives of delegated tasks—and that includes identifying when to bring issues to the project leader. Regular team meetings help keep the entire team on the same page.

**Trust.** Managers must trust staff to perform their assigned work. The leader can't micromanage, but they also cannot just walk away. The leader needs to be responsible for overall workflow and progress monitoring, and they must be available for questions. But employees must be allowed to own their part of the project fully, with no excuses.

Done effectively, delegation saves the project manager a ton of stress and grief. Here's a personal example demonstrating how . . .

In 2003, when I obtained my Professional Engineer

license and left the Department of Transportation, I was assigned my first project management position at a private engineering firm. As I've said before, implementation and management are two different things. I was used to designing my own plans and preparing cost estimates and specifications, but now my position required me to manage the entire project: oversee the progress of the staff engineers; manage the budget, schedule, and quality control; maintain relationships with clients; and develop project proposals to bring in new work.

My ego did not allow me to see past my own training and education, and I felt as though I had to do everything myself. I trusted no one with any major task! Well, you can guess the rest of the story: things started to fall through the cracks, and I got a major tongue-lashing from the principal of the firm.

"Well," I responded, "I can only work twelve- to sixteen-hour days for so long. What do you expect from me?"

I was lectured—in detail—that I was no longer a project engineer and that I'd better learn how to delegate those responsibilities.

Until this time, I'd been reluctant to turn over any responsibilities to the design staff, because I'd rather do it myself (again, I simply didn't trust them). However, from a time and position standpoint, what I was doing wasn't working either. Like Moses, I got advice from a more seasoned project manager: I humbled myself and asked for help. We went to lunch and discussed my situation, and we formed a plan to engage the staff, looked at workflows, and so on.

I then had to do what project managers do all the time: communicate to the staff what the expectations were. Needless to say, after some time, while the staff executed our various projects, I was able to spend more time on proposals, scheduling client meetings, and obtaining more work for the firm.

My stress fell as fast as I had picked it up. Getting good counsel is important, and no one is above asking for assistance.

## REFLECTION QUESTIONS

+ Where have you missed opportunities to delegate assignments as necessary?
+ Where has your ego gotten in the way of your seeing possible project efficiencies?
+ What resources could you use in your current situation to help you become a better delegator, e.g., staff, funding, workflow meetings, collaborations?
+ How can you learn to use the "spirit of counsel" to shore up your weak points and help you see things from a new perspective?
+ When have you succeeded in delegating? What were the benefits of doing so?

# Principle 6: Change Management

*Change management must be intentional. If you try to do too much, if you try to go too fast, if you don't inform people of the "why," you will lose your followers and the intended change will not succeed.*

## THE BIBLICAL PERSPECTIVE

Any type of change has a physical reaction in the human body. If the desired change is introduced too fast, it will most likely be met with stiff resistance. At the end of the day, accountability comes back to you as the leader. If you try to do it all yourself, you will fail—remember that you don't know everything. It is imperative to get the team on board.

I can't stress enough how important a project charter is when beginning any new project or endeavor—we need a vision of what must be done. We see how important this is in the book of Habakkuk 2:2–3 as follows:

²Then the Lord answered me and said:

> "Write the vision
> And make it plain on tablets,
> That he may run who reads it.
> ³For the vision is yet for an appointed time;
> But at the end it will speak, and it will not lie.
> Though it tarries, wait for it;
> Because it will surely come,
> It will not tarry.

When the vision of the change needed is clear, it becomes easier to implement. Let's take a break from biblical analysis in this chapter and jump right into some practical project tips.

## THE PROJECT PERSPECTIVE

Whether you are making a change in job, finances, health, or relationships, the change must be intentional. Good leaders anticipate change and develop strategies to prepare their team for that change. While leaders are often the visionaries proposing change to make things better, for the good of the team, *everyone* must have a stake and a role in implementing the change.

In my experience, several key steps will help create successful change:

+ Provide a clear rationale.
+ Define clear action steps.
+ Communicate.
+ Check your ego.
+ Use emotional intelligence.

**Provide a clear rationale.** Change should not be implemented simply for change's sake. Nor should it be completed with bias for a particular person's benefit or preference. Change should be made to achieve some sort of improved result for the team or organization—more transparency, greater efficiency, higher customer satisfaction, a better relationship—whatever the improvement might be. By explaining the rationale—the "why"—it becomes easier to get others on board with making the change.

**Define clear action steps.** While your team may buy into the idea of change, if they don't know what to do, things will be a muddle. List your priorities for critical tasks, problems to solve, decisions to make. Create a timeline for completion of short-term and long-term goals and tasks. Make sure the right resources—people, technology, money, time—are available. Change management is often an iterative process, so it helps to make the planning process a collaborative effort.

**Communicate.** Communicate, communicate, communicate! Ideally much of this communication is in the form of meetings or other face-to-face discussions. The higher the stakes for the change, the more important the in-person communication. This level of communication is necessary to get buy-in on the vision from your staff, to get their help in implementation planning, and to get their *critique* of the changes. Remember that as a leader, you often have subject matter experts working for you who know more than you do and who will ultimately be the ones to carry out these initiatives. Listen to them!

**Check your ego.** Related to the idea of listening to the experts on your team, I can't stress enough how critical it is to check your ego at the door. Just because you may have an idea or the solution to a problem, you still must communicate with the team and seek out potential problems with implementation of the changes being requested.

You may also have to deal with bias or resistance from individual team members. They may have been with the organization a lot longer than you have and may have legitimate concerns about the approach being proposed. Or they may have seen the organization jump on the latest business fad so many times that they don't trust these types of efforts anymore. Set your ego aside and at least *try* to get to the bottom of the resistance. You might be surprised by what you find. You need all the facts before moving forward, and it certainly makes it easier to move forward once all the issues are placed on the table.

**Use emotional intelligence.** Back in the day, change was rolled out suddenly and abruptly to staff, and you either accepted it or you moved on. Those two options were the extent of your choice. In recent years, the concept of *emotional intelligence* (EI) has come to the fore in management and project management. Emotional intelligence is the ability to deal with one's own emotions and the emotions of others in an empathetic and skillful way. (And when I say "skillful," I don't mean "manipulative.") Using EI can help a project manager establish a connection with their team and deal with resistance and other issues in a more productive and collegial way.

For me, EI looks like checking in with my team and seeing how they are doing—even if it's simply inquiring about their family. Once in a while I hold a staff lunch and then give them the rest of the day off. I also try to keep outings fun and not so serious with the business of the day. I try to show an overall genuine concern for my staff. To me, this is operating the Kingdom way rather than the world's way.

All these change management tips might sound easy enough, but to be honest, it is just as easy to flounder. In one of my jobs, I inherited a bit of a mess and tried to move too quickly to clean it up. Hoo-boy, did I learn my lesson . . .

When I started a job in community development and infrastructure planning for a suburban community, I was dumbfounded by what my predecessor left. Project Management 101 says that a new leader has only thirty days to blame previous leadership before they must own all problems and take complete responsibility for any messes. So, I had a lot of work to do in a short time.

I had several hot-button issues to resolve. First, the department was not a high-revenue-generating department, so we had limited resources to work with. Second, there was no clear policy for developers to follow for getting occupancy permits and paying the correct fees. Third, there was no comprehensive plan to define community initiatives around land use development, infrastructure priorities, housing, and so on. Worst of all, the department staff were not enthusiastic to have yet another group of managers coming in, along with an entirely new administration, all with their own ideas of how things should be done.

This of course provided for, shall we say, a less-than-ideal work environment. To top it off, we were in the middle of a worldwide pandemic, and staff were in and out of the office, often working remotely. Needless to say, a bad set of circumstances. (I bet you can relate.)

My first task was to prioritize the critical issues (as you can see, there were many). I literally made a list of all the issues and prayed to the Most High for the wisdom described in Habakkuk 2:2–3. Once the answer was "downloaded" to me, I proceeded to implement the plan.

However, old habits die hard, and I'm the type of individual who wants results not just now but *right* now! I proceeded to implement some of the changes immediately without much consultation, and several of the staff felt threatened, which led to a few very heated discussions. Thankfully, there is safety in a multitude of counsel, and my deputy director at the time convinced me that the steak dinner I wanted to serve up couldn't be swallowed whole but needed to be served in courses.

She was correct, and after numerous meetings and discussions, leadership and staff got on the same page. Once we did, our department went from $650,000 to $2.1 million in annual revenue; we created a comprehensive plan in seven months, when normally it would take twelve to fifteen months; we created a pavement management plan to rate all the streets and prioritize the repairs; we were able to add staff; and we had a much better work environment.

Organizations rise or fall based on the strengths or weaknesses of their leadership and management teams. Empathy and emotional intelligence are musts for implementing change and achieving results.

## REFLECTION QUESTIONS

+ In your realm, what are some challenges to effective change management that could arise unexpectedly?
+ How in your own life or work have you been resistant to change? How has your resistance hindered you from moving forward?
+ What tools do you find most effective in implementing the change management process?

+ What metrics do you use to measure the
  effectiveness of the change?
+ When have you succeeded at introducing a large
  change? What did you do that enabled adoption of
  that change?

# PRINCIPLE 7: TEACHABILITY

*We must be teachable. When we discover truths we have not been aware of, we must be ready to pivot and change course.*

## THE BIBLICAL PERSPECTIVE

Human beings are who they are primarily due to three basic things: observation, association, and teaching. We receive principles from parents, relatives, religious and educational institutions, and society at large. The intent of a teaching might have been benign, but sometimes the results are less than stellar. Recall from chapter 1 that we have an enemy called Satan, who is the god of this world system and wants to shape our thoughts and actions to his own ends rather than based on truth. When we discover truths we have not been aware of, if we want the results of true knowledge, we must be ready to pivot immediately and change course.

Additionally, as we've discussed, different positions (technical expert, manager, leader) require different skill sets. I've seen people in my professional career leave jobs because of having to work with people in roles they had no business occupying. We must keep learning, and the key is to renew your mind to the truth of God's word. As Romans 12:2 says, "And do not be conformed to this world, but be transformed by the renewing of your mind, that you may prove what is that good and acceptable and perfect will of God."

To help bring these concepts to light, let's look at Mark 4:1–20 for the grandaddy of all parables, the parable of the sower. I trust that this truth will be profound.

[1] And again He began to teach by the sea. And a great multitude was gathered to Him, so that He got into a boat and sat in it on the sea; and the whole multitude was on the land facing the sea. [2] Then He taught them many things by parables, and said to them in His teaching:

[3] "Listen! Behold, a sower went out to sow. [4] And it happened, as he sowed, that some seed fell by the wayside; and the birds of the air came and devoured it.

⁵ Some fell on stony ground, where it did not have much earth; and immediately it sprang up because it had no depth of earth. ⁶ But when the sun was up it was scorched, and because it had no root it withered away. ⁷ And some seed fell among thorns; and the thorns grew up and choked it, and it yielded no crop. ⁸ But other seed fell on good ground and yielded a crop that sprang up, increased and produced: some thirtyfold, some sixty, and some a hundred."

⁹ And He said to them, "He who has ears to hear, let him hear!"

¹⁰ But when He was alone, those around Him with the twelve asked Him about the parable. ¹¹ And He said to them, "To you it has been given to know the mystery of the Kingdom of God; but to those who are outside, all things come in parables, ¹² so that

> 'Seeing they may see and not perceive,
> And hearing they may hear and not understand;
> Lest they should turn,
> And their sins be forgiven them.'"

¹³ And He said to them, "Do you not understand this parable? How then will you understand all the parables? ¹⁴ The sower sows the word. ¹⁵ And these are the ones by the wayside where the word is sown. When they hear, Satan comes immediately and takes away the word that was sown in their hearts. ¹⁶ These likewise are the ones sown on stony ground who, when they hear the word,

immediately receive it with gladness; [17] and they have no root in themselves, and so endure only for a time. Afterward, when tribulation or persecution arises for the word's sake, immediately they stumble. [18] Now these are the ones sown among thorns; they are the ones who hear the word, [19] and the cares of this world, the deceitfulness of riches, and the desires for other things entering in choke the word, and it becomes unfruitful. [20] But these are the ones sown on good ground, those who hear the word, accept it, and bear fruit: some thirtyfold, some sixty, and some a hundred."

Okay, let's unpack this parable . . .

Human beings are the only creatures on this planet that are self-programmable. We are designed that way by the Most High God. We are "speaking spirits"—creators by nature. When a principle or concept is introduced to us, we have the ability to grab it, meditate on it, and work on it until the principle becomes reality in our lives.

As managers, parents, spouses, businesspeople, and so on, we are often faced with needing to make major improvements in our lives. But, because of old habits, that's often not easy to do. That is, the observation, association, and teaching that we've obtained previously may run counter to the new truths we are trying to manifest. Let's be clear: for any situation—salvation, healing, financial increase, relationships—the "seed" is the word of the Most High God.

The first group mentioned in the parable get the life-changing word (the seeds sown by the sower) stolen by Satan immediately. I would venture that these folks aren't really serious about what they are hearing, and it goes in one ear and out the other. They attend conferences, church, and seminars—maybe with the intention of learning something but without it being very high on their priority list.

The second group of folks are the most unfortunate, in my mind. They actually have intentions of making changes with the information they receive, but they refuse to elevate their thinking above this world system. When Satan brings pressures to their lives, they get offended, think that they are wasting their time, and drop the word altogether. A root of bitterness can also set in as they fail to realize that everything in this life starts from the spiritual before it translates to the natural. Satan controls the five senses and the systems in the physical world, so we must rise above that not only to obtain great knowledge but also to apply it and get the proper results.

The third group of folks are similar to the second group, as they allow distractions and procrastination to keep them from meditating on the concept or principle to get the required results. Make no mistake: when we decide to make life-altering changes—whether becoming born again, losing weight, or getting out of debt—it takes work, and you must be hungry for the change. There are no magic bullets. The Most High has given humanity the ability to choose good or evil, life or death, blessings or cursings! Ultimately, we must eliminate distractions and focus solely on the manifestations of the word sown.

The final group of those who increased thirty-, sixty- and a hundred-fold were able to hold the line and to follow through on the word. These are our true leaders in society. (However, the Most High is no respecter of persons. Verse 12 says that at any time, a person can have their sins forgiven and be converted to the Kingdom of God, so no one is better than anyone else.) These are the ones who have decided to do what is necessary to have victory; they have ignored distractions and everything else that automatically comes when you are looking for a breakthrough. Even the increase they experience—thirty-, sixty-, or a hundred-fold—is based on their individual capacity to receive and execute.

## THE PROJECT PERSPECTIVE

Being teachable shows up in numerous places in life— everywhere from work to relationships to sports and recreational activities.

For instance, have you ever noticed how some NBA teams with strong players barely end up making the playoffs? It's a head-scratcher, but I believe it goes back to coaching. As a coach (the leader), your job is to make sure the pieces fit together and function correctly. You literally need to "sow the vision" again and again so the team can buy into a system that will end up benefiting everyone. For example, you may need to stress, "Player A, you don't get to make all the shots, and, Player B, you may need to share your minutes or even come off the bench." Phil Jackson, head coach of the six-time NBA champion Chicago Bulls, was a master of coaching and teaching. He had a lot of superstars (with big egos) who at first didn't work well together. Over time, once his vision was made plain and the players trusted him and became teachable, the Bulls became one of the most dominant teams in the history of the league.

Becoming teachable and learning new concepts, skills, and principles may require prayer or meditation, analysis of resources, and an honest reflection on your own strengths and weaknesses as a leader or manager. It may also require you to read more or to attend leadership seminars to get new insights. Of course, clear metrics and regular communication with your team (whether that's colleagues or family or friends) can help track your progress. And progress will sometimes come rapidly and sometimes take years . . .

My senior year at Northwestern University, I was full of anticipation—for graduation day and getting the heck out of Dodge and keeping what was left of my brain intact! Senior civil engineering students had a class called Special Transportation Projects. Professor Joseph L. Schofer (now emeritus) was well known in the department and to this day still consults on major transportation projects. We had a total of three projects for the class: a realignment and feasibility study of the CTA elevated line on the west side (called the Green Line), a hospital heliport retrofit at Evanston Hospital, and a rideshare feasibility study for the parking lots at Northwestern University. (As it happens, all these projects were direct application projects and ended up getting published.)

But by the time we got to senior year and then only a month or two away from graduation, we were worn out. We wanted to travel from Evanston to Chicago to party and relax. In our Green Line feasibility study, there were five of us in the project group, along with a teaching assistant (TA). Each one of us had our own part to complete, and then we were supposed to make a presentation to the professor. We spent a few days on the report, presented the project, and went about our business, feeling pretty good about our end product.

Well, a few days later we came back and were completely shocked when we got our grades back: we all got a B. "What gives?" I asked the professor.

He said something I'll never forget: "Your research was excellent, but you spent zero time putting together the presentation. It was disjointed and sloppy." He didn't stop there. "When you are in public, you are in front of lay people. They don't speak engineering, but they are in charge of approval." He was especially hard on the grad student TA, saying to her, "You of all people should have known better."

Civil engineers (and engineers in general) are not historically known as great writers or speakers. Engineers tend to have tunnel vision and spend too much time analyzing issues. Our professor had said from the beginning to make the presentation as though we were speaking to grade-schoolers, but I was upset and had a hard time really listening to what he said.

I didn't readily receive the "seed" that the professor was sowing in us for later in our careers. I had to work for years to learn to write and speak clearly but not too technically. Nevertheless, over time, as I practiced, I slowly became more and more trusted in my field, and the "seed" increased a hundred-fold as designed.

## REFLECTION QUESTIONS

+ What actions have you failed to take to receive the "seed" in your life? Consider both the spiritual and nonspiritual "seeds."
+ How have distractions gotten you off course from achieving your goals?
+ Where have you succeeded in accepting the "seed"—spiritual or otherwise—and received the positive results from doing so?

# Principle 8: Discernment

*We must develop discernment. Discernment provides good judgment and guidance that supersedes human understanding.*

## THE BIBLICAL PERSPECTIVE

Now that we've discussed how a person receives the "seed" and becomes teachable, let's discuss a related concept: discernment. Recall, we defined discernment earlier as the ability to judge or perceive something that is not obvious, as well as spiritual guidance and understanding that supersedes human knowledge and understanding.

In Genesis, we can see how this concept helped Jacob in dealing with his father-in-law, Laban. Laban was borderline wicked: Jacob wanted to marry one of his daughters and Laban tricked him into marrying a different daughter; then Laban changed Jacob's wages multiple times; and then he forced Jacob into a twenty-year obligation, just to get his own wealth and independence and be able to leave. Sound familiar? Most folks face inflation, the cost of living, and seemingly never being able to get ahead in life in this world system run by you-know-who. So what are we to do? We need wisdom and discernment.

Jacob had a covenant with the Most High God that he would be on top, the head and not the tail, above only and not beneath, the lender and not the borrower (see Deuteronomy 28:1–15). Let's look at **Genesis 30:25–43** to see how Jacob used that covenant and discernment to deal with Laban:

25 And it came to pass, when Rachel had borne Joseph, that Jacob said to Laban, "Send me away, that I may go to my own place and to my country. 26 Give me my wives and my children for whom I have served you, and let me go; for you know my service which I have done for you."

27 And Laban said to him, "Please stay, if I have found favor in your eyes, for I have learned by experience that the Lord has blessed me for your sake." 28 Then he said, "Name me your wages, and I will give it."

<sup>29</sup> So Jacob said to him, "You know how I have served you and how your livestock has been with me. <sup>30</sup> For what you had before I came was little, and it has increased to a great amount; the Lord has blessed you since my coming. And now, when shall I also provide for my own house?"

<sup>31</sup> So he said, "What shall I give you?"

And Jacob said, "You shall not give me anything. If you will do this thing for me, I will again feed and keep your flocks: <sup>32</sup> Let me pass through all your flock today, removing from there all the speckled and spotted sheep, and all the brown ones among the lambs, and the spotted and speckled among the goats; and these shall be my wages. <sup>33</sup> So my righteousness will answer for me in time to come, when the subject of my wages comes before you: every one that is not speckled and spotted among the goats, and brown among the lambs, will be considered stolen, if it is with me."

<sup>34</sup> And Laban said, "Oh, that it were according to your word!" <sup>35</sup> So he removed that day the male goats that were speckled and spotted, all the female goats that were speckled and spotted, every one that had some white in it, and all the brown ones among the lambs, and gave them into the hand of his sons. <sup>36</sup> Then he put three days' journey between himself and Jacob, and Jacob fed the rest of Laban's flocks.

<sup>37</sup> Now Jacob took for himself rods of green poplar and of the almond and chestnut trees, peeled white

strips in them, and exposed the white which was in the rods. ³⁸ And the rods which he had peeled, he set before the flocks in the gutters, in the watering troughs where the flocks came to drink, so that they should conceive when they came to drink. ³⁹ So the flocks conceived before the rods, and the flocks brought forth streaked, speckled, and spotted. ⁴⁰ Then Jacob separated the lambs, and made the flocks face toward the streaked and all the brown in the flock of Laban; but he put his own flocks by themselves and did not put them with Laban's flock.

⁴¹ And it came to pass, whenever the stronger livestock conceived, that Jacob placed the rods before the eyes of the livestock in the gutters, that they might conceive among the rods. ⁴² But when the flocks were feeble, he did not put them in; so the feebler were Laban's and the stronger Jacob's. ⁴³ Thus the man became exceedingly prosperous, and had large flocks, female and male servants, and camels and donkeys.

Let's summarize, shall we?

Jacob was making Laban rich because God's blessing was on Jacob, but Jacob was suffering because he couldn't get ahead. He was being tricked out of his wages, and he got tired of it (sound familiar?). So, he needed discernment to get out of the situation; he couldn't do it naturally. He needed the biblical mechanics of operating in the Kingdom of the Most High God.

Now, I want to warn you that sometimes the answers we receive through discernment don't make sense to the natural mind, but they make *faith*. Jacob asked for all of the sheep that were recessive in genetic makeup (spotted and speckled); those would be Jacob's, and Laban would have all of the "normal"-looking sheep. Laban must have thought, *What a dummy!* However, the tables were turned when Jacob's flock produced the strongest spotted and speckled sheep, and Laban's produced weaker "normal" sheep. To the natural mind this made absolutely no sense, but as a result, Jacob ended up developing wealth that far exceeded Laban's. Discernment was the key to getting the answer Jacob needed, and it was supernatural!

We all have the ability to get the wisdom of the Most High—if we can believe. As James 1:5–8 says:

> [5] If any of you lacks wisdom, let him ask of God, who gives to all liberally and without reproach, and it will be given to him. [6] But let him ask in faith, with no doubting, for he who doubts is like a wave of the sea driven and tossed by the wind. [7] For let not that man suppose that he will receive anything from the Lord; [8] he is a double-minded man, unstable in all his ways.

This concept is applicable in every area of life and is a great equalizer. Whether other folks have more education, more financial resources, and so on, it makes no difference.

## THE PROJECT PERSPECTIVE

I personally believe that you can get discernment (wisdom) anytime you need it and for any situation. But first and foremost, you must be willing to think outside the box. This is not just a simple catchphrase—it will begin to separate you from the pack.

First, look at your current resources, and use the tools that already work. This may be trial-and-error at first, but eventually the fine-tuning will come. Then, learn to address every challenge as an opportunity to establish your vision for a successful outcome. This will help you become a skilled problem-solver. As part of your growth process, learn to open yourself up to unexpected solutions. Let me share an example of what I mean.

As community development director, I was tasked with annual infrastructure planning and management, which encompassed projects like road resurfacing, water mains, and sewer maintenance as well as any state or county projects that affected the town. One year, one of the biggest issues we dealt with was street resurfacing: which streets would get completed? We had limited funds, and it became a political issue (surprise, surprise).

I realized that priority based on a loose assessment and general preference would not work, because with seventy-five lane-miles of local streets, each subdivision or local homeowners' association would complain that they were overlooked and would eventually call the administration on the carpet regarding the selection process.

My solution was to come up with a community-wide street rating system that was neutral and would provide the needed information, and that also used solid empirical evidence that no one could challenge.

Once again, funding was a limiting factor in how many streets we could repair. On top of that, we were still in the middle of COVID-19 restrictions.

After I looked at the situation and asked God for wisdom, the solution came to my remembrance: a pavement management plan funded 100 percent by a third-party company, utilizing motor-fuel tax dollars. This was funding allocated to each town in the state based on population and lane-miles; in other words, we didn't need to pay for this project out of our regular funds.

Not only did we get all of the studies done, but we also created a detailed report that showed an overall condition rating for each street as well as the funding needed for repairs per lane-mile. Also, I remembered the advice from my Northwestern professor about making sure my presentation was detailed but simple enough to not talk over the heads of the administration.

Long story short, this solution became the process used annually, and for full transparency, the information is made available on the town's website. Not bad for wisdom at work!

## REFLECTION QUESTIONS

+ How can wisdom and discernment be applied to your projects and everyday issues?
+ How have you missed a solution by being biased toward the facts and resources at hand? Are you more God-conscious or world-conscious when attacking problems?
+ Where have you succeeded in discerning unexpected solutions?

# Principle 9: Faith

*With faith, we can overcome obstacles.*
*Even skilled managers hit obstacles.*
*Finding solutions means having faith, using*
*discernment, and being open to creative and*
*sometimes seemingly illogical solutions.*

## THE BIBLICAL PERSPECTIVE

Life is full of challenges, and solutions can sometimes seem impossible to find. It is in these instances that we must go against our natural mind, training, and the fact-based world and instead depend on faith. When we do so, faith can override time, space, and matter, and help us accomplish in a very short amount of time what would normally take an extended period.

Let's look at the miraculous draught of fishes (when Jesus first called his disciples), which is the first example of management by the anointing. (Recall that anointing was defined earlier as the empowerment to prosper, or the ability to override time, space, and matter.) From the Gospel of Luke 5:1–11:

1 So it was, as the multitude pressed about Him to hear the word of God, that He stood by the Lake of Gennesaret, 2 and saw two boats standing by the lake; but the fishermen had gone from them and were washing their nets. 3 Then He got into one of the boats, which was Simon's, and asked him to put out a little from the land. And He sat down and taught the multitudes from the boat.

4 When He had stopped speaking, He said to Simon, "Launch out into the deep and let down your nets for a catch."

5 But Simon answered and said to Him, "Master, we have toiled all night and caught nothing; nevertheless at Your word I will let down the net." 6 And when they had done this, they caught a great number of fish, and their net was breaking. 7 So they signaled to their partners in the other boat to come and help them. And they came and filled both the boats, so that they began to sink. 8 When Simon Peter saw it, he fell down at Jesus' knees, saying, "Depart from me, for I am a sinful man, O Lord!"

9 For he and all who were with him were astonished

at the catch of fish which they had taken; [10] and so also were James and John, the sons of Zebedee, who were partners with Simon. And Jesus said to Simon, "Do not be afraid. From now on you will catch men." [11] So when they had brought their boats to land, they forsook all and followed Him.

Let's break this down, shall we? Simon Peter was definitely an experienced fisherman by trade. Like most of us, he surely worked hard to become trained in his profession. However, there are times when we all hit a brick wall, and all our background and training is not enough to solve a problem. The scripture says Simon had "toiled all night and caught nothing." Simon probably had payroll to meet and people who were counting on him to bring in some fish and bolster the local economy, so the pressure was certainly on.

It's interesting that whenever Jesus taught, he immediately demanded faith in action of his followers. When Jesus told Simon to let down his nets, Simon's response was typical of someone who was just frustrated and angry: "Dude, we've been doing that already!" (I imagine he gave an eyeroll here.) "Whatever . . . we'll give it a shot." Simon's response was half-hearted at best. In other words, "Let me see if this 'faith' stuff really works."

You know the rest of the story: Simon Peter's net broke from the weight of all those fish, he called for his partners, their net broke, and they caught something like an entire year's supply of fish in one day! Simon was astounded. Once again, faith and the anointing *acted upon* yielded supernatural results.

Let's step back for a moment before we conclude. I have noticed that the Most High has a strange sense of humor. I know you're thinking, *Not the Most High God of the universe?* Yes. Stay with me (see Psalms 2 when God sits in the heavens and laughs at the devices of natural man). Some of God's humor:

+ Marching around a wall for seven days and then the walls fall down flat.
+ Curing a skin disease by washing in a dirty river.
+ Fishing in the daytime (when everyone knows that's totally ridiculous).
+ Declaring in the middle of a famine that tomorrow food will be plenty and cheap.
+ Reducing an army of 30,000 to 300 to defeat an entire foreign nation.

I could go on and on.

What am I getting at? When you are looking for true breakthrough in any area of life, the Most High certainly wants to answer your prayer of petition, but in most cases the methods are nonsensical to the natural mind. He is breaking down our natural reasoning because he is not limited by anything. To get God's best, we sometimes must be willing to look a bit foolish to the world and not be concerned about it. He not only wants to give us the answer but also to break down any high-mindedness or arrogance we may have. The Most

High is concerned about our total development. This is a key principle of biblical mechanics: the natural mind cannot comprehend the things of God (I Corinthians 2:14–16).

## THE PROJECT PERSPECTIVE

Once you start tapping into faith and getting creative, the things you need will start coming to you. Help is available—you don't have to do everything yourself. We've all had projects that were well thought out and planned but just seemed to run into roadblocks at every turn: the project goes over budget, there are seemingly unsolvable technical problems, the schedule gets blown, the stakeholders are upset at the current progress (or lack thereof). This is when the anointing kicks in because "faith comes by hearing, and hearing by the word of God" (Romans 10:17). Let me share how faith helped me solve a difficult problem.

When I joined a mid-size municipal engineering firm that managed infrastructure projects for local municipalities, it was just after the Great Recession of 2008–2009, and local communities had been especially affected. I was assigned to a mid-size suburban community. My director of engineering told me that this community was at the bottom of annual revenue for our company and that I shouldn't expect much in the way of new projects. I was always about hustling and making it happen despite less-than-ideal circumstances, so that statement didn't sit well with me. I noticed that we had several plans and studies for various projects—roadway improvements, sewer repairs, comprehensive plan development—just sitting on the shelf. I knew these were worthy projects and would improve the community, if only we could find funding for them. This was important to me, as I was the only African American professional engineer on staff in the entire company, and I certainly did not want to get stuck with a constantly "nonperforming" community.

So, I prayed and meditated and the miracle of the big draught of fish came to my mind. The funding was there all the time, but my "personal recognition system"—my PRS—was out of alignment. *What is a PRS?* you may ask. It's like an internal GPS—and a form of anointing from the Most High. (Credit for this concept goes to my pastor and teacher, Dr. Bill Winston at Living Word Christian Center, Forest Park, Illinois.) I was thinking only in three dimensions, not four.

I focused my prayer and meditation on how we could get the funding for these projects. A few days later, a good friend of mine came to mind. Valencia Williams was a professor at Purdue University who had recently been hired as the grants manager at my company. Something told me to reach out to her, and when we eventually had lunch, I shared my dilemma about funding all these projects.

As you can probably guess, with Ms. Val's expertise

in grant writing and my shovel-ready projects with budgets and scopes at the ready, we ended up with about $20 million in funding for projects over the next five years. This nonperforming community went from the bottom of the revenue list up to becoming one of the top five communities in the entire company.

The following year, when we had our company retreat and the news got out about the abrupt change in revenue from this "problem" community, every municipal engineer asked me how I was able to achieve the turnaround, especially in such a dry economic climate. My response: I called for my partners and strategized! It was prayer and meditation as well as waiting on the answer from the Most High. I was simply willing to let down my professional "nets" for a great draught of "fish." Now this funding model is used not only in that particular firm, but it has become a standardized model region-wide.

Just drop the nets.

## REFLECTION QUESTIONS

+ What is holding you back from walking by faith?
+ What actions will you take to make the shift from "sense knowledge" to "faith activation"?
+ When have you "dropped your nets" and experienced a great draught?

# The Conclusion of the Matter

As you can see, the idea of biblical mechanics is vast. There are too many examples to cover in this book, but these principles are foundational to mastering this life we have. The Most High God expects us to provide a proper return on investment and to impact the world accordingly.

I believe we are currently suffering from a lack of knowledge and a lack of strong moral principles—not just among the people of God but in the world at large. Jesus Christ (the anointed one and his anointing) gave humanity a guide to follow and has empowered humankind to be successful and prosperous utilizing biblical mechanics.

Let's summarize the basic but profound principles in this book:

Everyone on this planet is a manager of someone and/or something, no matter how small or large. There are no excuses for not executing our mandate on this earth. The question is, which system of operation will we use: the world system, which operates based on our five physical senses along with observation, association, or teaching, and which is always bound to fall short of the goals of excellence, or the Kingdom of God system?

Our biggest obstacle to operating with excellence within the Kingdom of God system is a soul issue—meaning the mind, will, emotions, intellect, or imagination (see III John 2). The soul connects the spirit and body, and if any one of its elements is not operating in the truth, it is equivalent to having a kink in the hose. It used to frustrate me that on a hot summer's day, when we would drink out of a garden hose, if there was a kink anywhere in the line, the water would just drip out, even though the pressure was on full force. Only after we found the kink and removed it would the water come out fast—sometimes to the surprise of the person on the receiving end! That is how our soul operates. If we've been wounded with past hurts and trauma, the flow cannot get through because of our soul condition. Once we clear the kinks, watch the power flow like a raging river!

We must be honest about our shortcomings and mistakes. We shouldn't hide from responsibility, nor run in the "Victim Olympics" (blaming others for everything that goes wrong in our lives). We don't want to be like the guy with one talent in the parable of the talents who, when called on the carpet to give an account of why he failed to execute his assignment, immediately started pointing fingers at everyone and everything instead of taking personal responsibility for his actions. We need to be quick to repent (meaning to return to God or to completely change one's mind about a situation).

Check your ego at the door! You may look eccentric or even foolish at times when executing these principles, but again, we are *not* operating out of sense knowledge or education. Rather we are tapping into the truth, which will put us high above our circumstances and situations.

All these principles operate by *faith*! Hebrews 11:6 says, "But without faith, it is impossible to please Him, for he who comes to God must believe that He is, and that he is a rewarder of those who diligently seek Him." Notice the word "diligently" in the verse. That means we need to be consistently consistent. It is a lifestyle, not a fad or the latest craze. Only when we operate in such truth and power will we see the results described in this writing.

I hope you found some nuggets in this book that you can apply right away. Let us all make an effort to strive to be better in all areas of life, no matter our background, situation, or circumstances, as we all can master the law of biblical mechanics.

# About the Author

ERNEST R. ROBERTS III has spent thirty-plus years working in the public and private sectors and has both design and construction engineering experience. He's been a municipal engineer for several towns, managing infrastructure budgets and long-range planning, and is currently the Director of Community Development and Infrastructure Planning for the Village of Matteson, Illinois. He holds a Bachelor of Science degree in civil engineering from Northwestern University and is a licensed Professional Engineer (PE) and certified Project Management Professional (PMP).